EUROPE

MORE FROM THE EMMA PRESS

POETRY PAMPHLETS

how the first sparks became visible, by Simone Atangana Bekono,
tr. from Dutch by David Colmer
do not be lulled by the dainty starlike blossom, by Rachael Matthews
With others in your absence, by Zosia Kuczyńska
Sandsnarl, by Jon Stone
This House, by Rehema Njambi
is, thinks Pearl, by Julia Bird
What the House Taught Us, by Anne Bailey
Overlap, by Valerie Bence
The Fabulanarchist Luxury Uprising, by Jack Houston
The Bell Tower, by Pamela Crowe
Ovarium, by Joanna Ingham
Milk Snake, by Toby Buckley

SHORT STORIES

The Secret Box, by Daina Tabūna, tr. from Latvian by Jayde Will
Tiny Moons: A year of eating in Shanghai, by Nina Mingya Powles
Postcard Stories 2, by Jan Carson
Hailman, by Leanne Radojkovich

BOOKS FOR CHILDREN

My Sneezes Are Perfect, by Rakhshan Rizwan,
illustrated by Benjamin Phillips
The Bee Is Not Afraid of Me: A Book of Insect Poems,
edited by Fran Long and Isabel Galleymore
Cloud Soup, by Kate Wakeling, illustrated by Elīna Brasliņa

ART SQUARES

Menagerie, by Cheryl Pearson, illustrated by Amy Louise Evans
One day at the Taiwan Land Bank Dinosaur Museum,
written and illustrated by Elīna Eihmane
Pilgrim, by Lisabelle Tay, illustrated by Reena Makwana
The Fox's Wedding, by Rebecca Hurst, illus. by Reena Makwana

Europe, Love Me Back

Rakhshan Rizwan

THE EMMA PRESS

THE EMMA PRESS

First published in the UK in 2022 by The Emma Press Ltd.
Poems © Rakhshan Rizwan 2022.
Cover design and interior illustrations © Reena Makwana 2022.

ISBN 978-1-912915-14-9

A CIP catalogue record of this book
is available from the British Library.

Printed and bound in the UK
by TJ Books, Padstow.

The Emma Press
theemmapress.com
hello@theemmapress.com
Birmingham, UK

Supported using public funding by
ARTS COUNCIL ENGLAND

CONTENTS

Bite

Summer is sudden
it bites the skin   the bare face on a lit-up stage
you can see details of the brickwork
the wide-open pores   that need closing
Your eyes are at their bluest   I can see
the sun begin to lighten your hair   I see
the freckles on your pink skin   the fleas on your dog
the garage doors with their paint chipped in places
the dried liquid on the lids of black garbage cans
On Fridays   I can see inside your house
the polish of new furniture   white flowers cascading
from empress trees and landing in the blonde hair
of your children   I can see the sunscreen
and the spray tan   the flaps of skin like parchment coils
documenting a life   storing the memory of each birth
At the community pool   a brown girl shouts at
a white boy   the commotion of wet feet
and paddling quietens down   everyone takes sides
I can see the gold ring   flashing in your nostril
I hear the children   splashing and singing *mandaag,*
dinsdag, woensdag, donderdag, vrijdag
I can see you swallow a lump   into the throat of history
as you see me   as you cross the road

I can see how you hang close to your friends
all the beautiful sundresses swishing   and your tall
children by your side   with their ice-creams
I can feel the lick of conversation on your tongues
history   a wish-bone   stuck in our throats
I am the most dressed person in the street
my skirt   a deep green   does not carry with the wind
a hijab tied into a summer turban will not toss in the wind
like a head of pale hair   I can see the fingers that never
touched my arm   the way your eyes avert just a little
how your voice loses its lilt   how you tighten your grasp
on your dog's leash   one day you will see the way
my skin pores open in the summer months
to receive warmth   same
as yours.

Adjunct

When a country is so shuttered in
how do you get it to open?

I knocked and I knocked but nobody answered.
The door of the university is heavy, leaden,
and does not swing open; it is made for bodies
different from my own,

I waited for a professor to lead me in, but nobody offered;
the door meanwhile became more gilded and beautiful
and triple my body weight.
I tried to slip my academic degrees in under the door;
my vaccination record, bank statements,
language certificates, integration exams,
tuberculosis test. I slipped in my CV and cover letter
and a recent photograph; a sonnet, a villanelle,
a short story (we fight back with paper
because we are civilized).
Someone told me to try other ways: pick the lock,
pry it open, but I did not want to be a brown crook
and prove them right

Instead I did a performance piece, tied myself
to a cardboard replica of the Gothic door

and carried it everywhere:
to the library, the bus, the train station,
wearing it even as I showered, ate,
Netflixed and chilled, performed literature reviews
and researched papers, but no one was interested
in eliciting my testimony. After all, I wasn't dead –
I wasn't ill – and hadn't this country treated me so well?

For it is not a human right to be much more
than Agamben's bare life, to exist in
the hallowed halls of the academe.
There comes a point when our wanting
is simply too much. Obscene.

Now I stand in the department's courtyard
where Mannekin Pis is playing
and I let the flecks of wind and vapour,
Europe's rarefied urine, cover me.

A hundred years of gaze

For the ashen-eyed imam her body is an aberration; it makes
sacred calligraphies tremble in shades of indigo and gold

for her neighbour she is a rosary-clutching fanatic,
her breath ponderous with ardent, syrupy Arabic

for passengers on the bus her body is a peg
to hang their eyeballs, en route to suburban hell

for her son she is songs in four languages, each one wrapped
around the other, hissing, silken, serpentine

for her professor she is otherness, the red of her embroidered dress
a chromatic invasion on a grey winter

for the hooded dog-walker crossing the street, she is
the clash of civilizations, the mortar from distant wars

the swollen bodies of refugees marking borderlands in the sea,
the Gothic need to be expunged from the European imaginary

all that is left whispering when the mind empties itself,
but her body is more   than something to move a slow news day

a signifier to light and take a long drag; more than
a Rumi verse, a nesting doll, a whirling Sufi, a harem girl –

she begins to cut herself out of dinner conversations, headlines,
starts to sew herself a brand new skin.

Half the Sin

At the break of day, nuns
from the parish of Saint Luke in Dublin,
begin ringing doorbells,
the rustle of their robes a slow-approaching storm
leaving windows, mouths, slightly askew.
In their arms, a child wrapped in muslin;
to help match likeness and limbs;
a midwife extracted from her house
at uncertain hours offers her hand,
her hand like a hook to pull out a sin
or a rope to throw to the drowning,
her hand which opened love letters
from fathers long gone to sea, or found
the remnants of an uncle's appetite
in the body of a quavering niece.
Her hand surgical, precise, separating
a dead twin from a living one,
blind without judgement
finding a couple's eleventh child
and delivering him to them, or discovering
death coiled, congealed inside warm tissue,
enclosed by the liquid of a beating heart,
or conversely pink, mewling tissue

in the mouth of a body, long-gone and blue.
But today her hand is a cross, a rubricated Bible
made from gold leaves. She covers her face,
extending only her unsteady hand.

Young women are lined up in the parlour –
Not her not her a mother protests. *She is nine.*
But her hand never discriminates: breasts are removed
from tight underclothes, breasts that have never known
this kind of touch, this kind of intrusion,
breasts that look surprised, indignant.
At last one leaks the milk of shame, with no ring in sight –
her liquid gold miraculous, life-giving.
The eyes of the townspeople become executioners
and talk gathers like frothy cream, rising above
the tip of a bone-china bowl ready to spill.

Two hundred years later, reading this Poor Law record,
I feel the quaint cocktail of a woman's hope
rise in my chest, feel my breasts harden
with milk, that peculiar ache of women's bodies
which do only half the sin
but carry all the history.

Medusa Ghosted

And when he left, she grew them inch by inch:
she brushed them with her fingers, wrapped them
in a Cashmere shawl; and when he didn't write,
she grew them; when he did, she grew them;
when he called, his voice gravelly and serious,
she was growing them; when she sat on a chair,
she sat on her hair, and when people's eyes slanted
she knew they stared at her luxurious black mane
which took half an hour to shampoo, ages to braid,
which smelled sad, wafted lavender while she slept.
And when she lost things, pins, promises,
they were almost always in her hair;
they enjoyed Monet's paintings,
Omar Khayyam's rubaiyat,
and the novels of Frederik van Eeden.

But when he returned unexpectedly, one July afternoon,
he didn't understand the hair. *Trim them a little,*
he suggested. *People are beginning to talk.*
Her hair turned an angry shade of crimson;
she had to untangle them strand by strand,
talk to them in soothing tones. *We don't trust him,*
they hissed, their forked tongues quivering.

Her mother massaged her hair with henna
and backcombed them shut;
She took her perfumed locks to his home;
slowly he pulled out all the pins. At first
he liked them: they tickled his feet, massaged his arms,
whispered sweet nothings in his ears, but soon
they were in the way: they got into his suits, his books,
they found their way into his collared shirts
and even his underpants; he found them glued
to the base of his throat, clinging to his skin,
smiling in his gravy. So he was glad to see them
falling in bunches after the baby came.
She carried the sad coils in her hands,
she buried them in their garden in white cardboard boxes,
she sang to them as they unravelled on her shoulders.
They cut themselves on soft cotton sheets, they lost their lives
in warm bathwater, until one day she decided
to put them out of their misery with a pair
of kitchen scissors
and stood in front of the mirror with an uneven bob,
hair like fish heads fallen in the sink,
martyrs in the cause, eyes silver and large.

Foundation in Rose Beige

– that is the name of skin that provides full coverage,
the name of the thing you say is *too much*, filling out
the pores, blemishes and scars, all the damaged women
sauntering around make-up counters,
dabbing it into their skin, rubbing it onto their bones,
my mother in the mirror squeezing out
a generous amount on her patriarchal wound,
women plastering their daughters
with foundation in Heavenly Honey.

Sometimes we need it up to our arms,
sometimes our thighs, sometimes we need to soak in it
to survive, sometimes we drink foundation in Suede Mocha,
keep it in our purses at all times, small vials of colour
tucked into our pillbox because we are bone setters,
shock absorbers, dirty dancers, ritual chanters,
healers, queens, magicians, conjurers, witches,
and we leave our Warm Vanilla on the pages we write,
the dishes we wash, the people we hold;
there are sutures of Deep Charmeuse on our faces,
stitches of paint, ointments of hue,
medicines in warm and cool shades;
there are prescriptions in Creamy Georgette

in our bathroom cupboards, doctor's orders in
Pink Bisque, holding us together as we tremble
in supermarket aisles, lie waiting on white hospital sheets.

Our mothers massaged Light Taffeta into our hair
before bidding us goodbye; the words spray-painted
on the subway walls are Soft Caramel,
the ink of our histories Golden Tan,
but sometimes my skin is Musty Ash:
then I am the darkest woman I have ever been.
My skin curdles and shows, my skin singed and burrowed
    and bone,
and I can no longer dab, no longer spread and mix.
I can no longer find a shade to swatch, stitch, suture and fix,
no longer even out the blots on this broken sheet of skin.

Flâneuse

She came from cities
where only men walked in the streets,
and women didn't
except to make themselves vulnerable
to men who wanted to kill them
for walking in the street.
She walked like a hallucination
of her own making,
as if she could scarcely believe she had a body.
She walked like a passenger chasing a train,
someone who wanted very much to be inanimate –
the hydrant, the café window, the bicycle stand –
to hide behind shadows and walls,
other people, her own gaze, winter coats.
She walked not to exist, but disappear, to be semi-visible.
The city wasn't built for her
so she had to trick it, make herself a shadow,
a spindly ghost, fit into the lapel of the city
or into its trouser pocket, and get away with it.

How does one walk in a city,
when the city was imagined for others?

The gazes seek her out,
letting her know she shouldn't be here,
but they fall softer on her skin
and she is learning to find herself
beneath all the words and the lessons
about space, size, men's legs.
Now all she needs are pockets to store her pepper spray,
and a lipstick that's secretly a knife.

Mindfulness

I'm not going to look in your window. I'm not.
Maybe you will invite me to dinner and maybe
you won't; I shouldn't obsess. I suggested it once
and texted you about it twice, but you're busy,
and that's enough. Your house is across the street,
Fontainbleaulaan 5. I know this because one time
we walked back together after dropping
the children at school and you told me about your life,
and about that car accident which really changed you.
It felt intimate. I felt like there was something there.
Would you like to grab a bite from the pizzeria,
Happy Italy? I'm here, pouring myself a cup of tea.
The sky is overcast but beautiful.
The brickwork of your house needs repair but
why do you pretend like we don't know each other?
I'm making pasta for us, and the children are playing
with bits of pasta, colouring them in with a marker.
I think about you, how you almost lost your son
in the crash, and fractured an arm.
You had dreams about it, for many nights afterwards.
I'm pouring in the sauce and it is starting to bubble,
but you can't come and I'm going to blame your husband.
I know how he looks at me, like he's deciding

if I'm fully human and hasn't made up his mind yet.
Yes it's not you, it's him. You and I are friends
in our minds, aren't we? We will order pizza
and watch a movie, maybe go for a walk,
the possibilities are endless.
I'm ordering lunch for myself now.
I think it might arrive cold.
I don't feel like pasta suddenly. I have lost my appetite,
and the light in your window has come on.
I don't know how you like your tea, as you never told me,
but I'm not thinking about any of this. I am moving away
from you and this and I am making space for other things.

(Incidentally, how many ribs did you break in the accident?)

Letter

I expect the postman to drop
anything into the mailbox:

a letter, a letter bomb or a petrol bomb,
a letter written in blood, anthrax or a love letter,
a phone number, a dinner invitation,
a notice of eviction or information about
a pending court date, an unpaid bill,
a tax notice, a rejected visa notification,
a permit extension deadline, a speeding ticket,
a deportation date, a murder threat, a yard sale,
an offer to wash the windows free of charge,
an upholsterer's address,
a verdict on the nationality application,
a tablet to administer in the event of
a nuclear holocaust, a neighbourhood stalker's letter,
a reminder from the city council to pay the water tax –

The emissary of this new country
is a minimum-wage messenger,
a messiah in orange overalls.

They say a thin letter means bad news;
you want a fat envelope,

a delicious letter with juicy news –
stab it with a fork
but watch out for parcels,
especially uneven ones
bound with string.

The scarlet letter found in my stomach
a free lottery ticket; the letter with the queen's seal
ripped me from the side, its hands shaking and white.
The speeding ticket found rage sleeping in my palms,
the unmarked bill opened me while holding its breath
and found the number of a collection agency
and an unpaid student loan coiled in my intestines.

She said

'What's going on?' the police officer said.
The neighbour had heard a child crying
and running down a stairwell, followed by
a man, angry, and a woman, pleading with him.

She knew this story well,
knew the things in their hearts:
deeds waiting in the melanated shadow,
to be committed

(what brown men do to brown women,
because of which they need saving by white women).
'You laughed in my fucking face when I came over
and asked you what was going on,' she said.

'We cannot be trusted with our own experiences,'
I said. 'We are unreliable narrators. We don't stick
to the script, have a bone to pick with the writer,
quibble with the plot and want to switch genres.'

I saw her crime thriller as a twisted comedy. She said,
'I won't speak to the man, but I am open to talking
to the woman.' She had found a victim, except
victims didn't laugh in the faces of their saviours

Victims didn't make the main character feel small,
foolish, bite-sized, full of misplaced rage and heroism.
There was a special place in hell, after all,
for victims who didn't act very victim-like.

And so, having lost patience with them both,
she called the police – who stood now
at the edge of the door, asking questions
about what was happening, who was doing what,

bringing a note from history, that we should never be
blissed out in the suburbs. A reminder to feel a little foreign
in our beds, in the arms of our lovers. Be grateful.
Be little immigrants, a touch accented, a bit alone.

My house is becoming like my country

My husband walks his pack of barge dogs past me every day,

I recite a prayer descending and ascending the stairs,

when the phone rings I jump, I hold my keys like a weapon,

I keep a photo identification with me at all times,

I smile at everyone in a uniform, there are tulips

growing in the living room (the former owner left bulbs

under the wooden floorboards), the kitchen is covered

in beautiful flora and fauna which we can't name,

things grow out of nothing and require no tending,

the earth is dark and rich and carries the scent of the ocean,

we are miles below sea level, one day we painted our faces

black, and now everything feels very strange between us,

black marionettes – zwarte pieten – swing from the walls

and traipse all over the house like trapeze artists,

sleep in the window displays and have such cheeky grins

but we don't know what any of this means. It isn't racism.

We clarified that over dinner. My son never vacates a seat

on the bus for me even though I am visibly pregnant.

No one speaks to me for days. I push my headscarf
further back into my bones but nothing changes.
One day my husband smiles at me and we have a
    conversation
and I change all my views about this house. I sleep in a bed
of tulips and all night the windmills waft perfume into
    my hair.
But then I go back to getting patted down every time
I need to take a piss, filing paperwork
before withdrawing anything from the refrigerator.
There is a border security officer in our bed,
he covers our bodies with exit/entry stamps
as we drift in and out of sleep, if anyone
as much as brushes against me in the corridor
I break into sweat. When I go to the attic
to bring down the laundry I have palpitations,
once someone came up behind me as I showered
and offered me loose change. My husband does not
    greet me
while bagging groceries, but he greets everyone else.

I notice everything. I am lying on the ground

and the ants are crawling over me. I am one with the earth.

I feel my spiritual chakras open. Nobody talks to me.

One day someone asks me for directions, I am sure

they are a serial killer. Last weekend we had guests over,

they talked and chatted with me in our bedroom

and before leaving one of them held me.

She smelled like coconut oil. Her hair fell in clumps

about her face, her stomach that familiar misshapen

protuberance from having birthed four children.

She reached into my back and counted

all the little curved bones. She said

You are beautiful, and in that moment I believed her.

I have found in my breast

a lump the size of King Bluetooth's treasure,
a small Damascus dirham at a beach in Rügen,
lying curled at the edges of Europe
underneath a flap of skin.

Get the Damascus out of Europe,
the Urdu from my mouth, the lump from my breast!
It is soft and sore and feels raw and flushed,
it is painful to touch but I don't want to visit
the doctor who finds my descriptions of pain
strange, exotic, exaggerated.
He sees a woman with too many words
of the wrong language in her mouth.

My breasts were dripping with milk last year.
All my maternal honey gathered around the rocks
and carved them smooth and soft brown,
and now they sag, the days are endless.
A woman died in this house, they will say,
her breasts eaten by lumps. No one caught them
because no one touched her. King Bluetooth's treasures
belonged to no one. What was her name?

She clawed at the teat of Europe, her body not meant
to be fed with the milk of the continent. She grew heavy
with malignancy and disease. What was her name?
The doctor will say, She never told me about the pain.
Her accent was distracting, an uninvited guest in her mouth.
She used all these words in English to describe it.
I would have asked: Is it relentless? Does it throb?
Is it intense, sharp, musical, a sonata in your marrow?

Basically, the Muslims are metastasizing
and this raw – gentle – constant – intermittent pain –
growing in intensity here, here, is in the body of Europe.
The painful lumps under the white sheets of skin
are cancer; do not touch her.

Petrarch

A fly in the sun, a fly on my nose,
a fly on a body that is mine in the sun,
a body rotting in a house on my nose in the sun –
the hair will take time to decompose
but the body will start to smell in the Dutch suburbs.

If a brown woman's body falls in a forest
and no one hears it, does it exist?
The fly is my mind, heavy in the sun –
overcooked, exhausted, flying around
a giant white suburban sinkhole of trimmed lawns,
 bicycles, and sundresses –
the fly is a memento mori;
his name, Petrarch, a wilful sonneteer,
terrified of prose.

In Translation

Sir, anything else? The waistcoated waiters
indulge their moustached Punjabi sahabs,
whose bottles of scotch gleam under their suits.
Niet nodig, I deliver with quivering tongue,
a rejoinder to the till girl's sharp blue eyes.

This thing called civilization, Tacitus wrote,
was really just part of being a slave.
The fatness of my tongue resists the prodding,
refuses to wrap itself around Ik ben this
and ik ben that. Two years ago, my German
grated against the impeccable standards of its owners
till it became sheer, wearable, like the finest chiffon.
Du kannst sehr gut Deutsch, they said,
and even though the sun warmed my face,
my skin lost its Pakistani tan, its berry browns.

But now, wrenching out these delicate sequins
of German articles, replacing sehr with zeer,
neun with negen, makes me want to escape
to my mother's Punjabi,
to the warm articulations of puttar aithay,
because when my grandfather said border-paar,

his wife didn't understand:
there was no word in Urdu for 'border',
which sent my grandmother into a tailspin –
not knowing the words lost her an entire country,
a portent for coming generations, when our tongues
insist on having the interview in Punjabi jee,
because our mouths cannot move beyond
our mothers' oily ghee and her puttar jee,
or speaking in Engels only because
in Nederlands we sound fragmented
by way of our speech,
our lives become precarious things.

Sir Syed insisted on taking the first swig:
he poured English into his mouth and cringed.
It always burns the first time, he said. Tastes like piss
but then the stillness comes quickly.
The fabric may snag on the jagged histories,
but at some point the scab becomes skin.
It's bitter medicine, not a vat of acid.
He called upon a sense of proportion to prevail.
I don't doubt the benefits, Sir Syed sahib.
I wouldn't dare. But India was never terra nullius –
my mother's Persian couplets
preceded her velvety Urdu.

That's all I wish to say to this thing called civilization:
if it would only step more carefully,
acknowledge the other bodies in the room,
novels littering the table, effaced scripts on the walls,
someone's love letters falling out of teak shelves,
perfumed scarves scattered on the bed,
unravelled turban on the floor.

A Man is speaking Urdu on the train and everyone is turning to look at him

Urdu is soft, apologetic, camouflaged,
but the difference in intonation
makes everyone look away, embarrassed.

The teenagers plug in their headphones,
avert their gaze; the ticket collector
approaches Urdu with caution.

This is the silent cabin, she says in Dutch.
Nahin, Nahin, Nahin, Urdu whispers
to a child who won't keep still.

Already Urdu is starting to breathe
down peoples' necks, already it is pouring
itself into their ears, running through the cabin,

clicking open all the windows, letting
the cold draught in. It runs down the walls,
drips into every conversation,

takes a sip of someone's morning coffee,
breaks a piece of bread, rings
like a giant church bell in a passing town.

In the end, it moves to the corner seats
and does not make eye contact.
It hangs from the body of its speaker

in beads of perspiration, crawls
into his tightening chest and grips
his skin till he switches to broken English.

Everyone makes space for the new visitor
with his uneven gait; they remove their luggage
from empty seats, and beckon him to sit.

Post-racial nation

In the doctor's office, waiting for our turn,
watching a tepid painting, a mediocre landscape
with too much blue; next to it, twelve pictures
of identical grey cats wearing dresses.

Between us there are boils and colds,
cancers in remission, economies in recession,
an itchy fungus, athlete's foot and endometriosis,
which will be dismissed as anxiety for another year.

We examine each other before he has us go
behind a curtain and quietly undress.
We take stock of the skin (its pallor), the cough
(its severity), the roughness of the nose.

We note the itch of your neck, the tick in your spine,
the crack of your knuckle, your hypochondria
accompanying you on this visit like a loyal friend.
We see when you cradle your belly.

Weren't you here, the last time I came?
How often do you need to show up?
Would you like an awkward conversation,
or will you browse a magazine from 2013?

Be well, the room says. You fill in your prescriptions.
Keep out of reach of children, shake well before use,
don't scratch after application,
in this post-racial nation.

My mother texts me at 6 am

Meri jaan, missing you. How are you?
I like the nail polish.
Your dresses are always so colourful.
Thanks for giving me a heads up.
Hey, dynamic soul.
Talk to me on Sunday, feeling lonely.
Thank you, my titly – butterfly.
Please wait a minute. I will call you back.
This is mama. I am always here for you
We have many blessings to celebrate.
This link is called Narcotics Anonymous
It's a support group for addicts
and it's supposed to be very helpful
Maybe you can attend meetings if he won't.
Please also discuss a recovery plan with his doctor.
It might be helpful to reach into community resources
Dil khush ker diya. You made my heart happy.
Meray dil kay tukron ko kisi ki nazar na lagay. I hope
the pieces of my heart are protected from the evil eye.
I got an exercise bike. Get one too.
I feel better.
You are so sweet. You comfort me through lovely gestures.
Your voice note made me smile.

I feel better.

7 truths about my addiction.

Is he okay? I just spoke to him
and he was talking a mile a minute.

Call me.

Love you more and more.

Enjoy your moments of achievement

He's a virus worse than corona!

Do you remember this train journey?

We went to Ipoh together

Sorry, it's late for you.

Hugs and loads of love

Maa ki jaan.

Goodnight, butterfly.

18th February, 1943

Sophie Scholl's thin wrists, the sharpness of the writing,
perspiration a drop in the heart of the nation,
its poisoned spleen, hurtling paper,
the caretaker catching a sinner in his line of sight.

'I am, now,' she writes, 'as before, of the opinion
that I did the best that I could do for my nation.
I, therefore, do not regret my conduct
and will bear the consequences
that result from my conduct.'

The guillotine, the hand, the pen and the papercut
compete in a contest of wits, but before that
she requests a last cigarette, a long drag
at the expense of the guards watching her,
shrinking years into short breaths
and seconds into a plume of smoke.

If the papers had fallen differently,
if she had reached her perch a moment earlier,
if the janitor had taken longer with his tea,
she would have run down the steps,
held Hans's hands and hurried out,
left the campus with the hundreds of students,
silent in their lecture halls.

She is a regular stop now on my way home,
where I must switch buses: Platz der Weissen Rose.
Her presence is suggested by a gentle ding
as passengers dismount, alight, recognize
the shift in the air, her seditious heart
beating in my body, this piece of history
I want to claim as an Auslander,
the only national narrative that makes sense to me.

Deflation

The mom whose spray tan
is the tangiest shade of orange
watches a giant jumping castle inflate,
watches all the children of the neighbourhood –
white shirts, blonde-brunette heads of hair,
scarlet cheeks – waiting for the slides and stairs
to become limber and full,
like the milk in the vanilla shakes
being passed around.
The only boy not invited
is mine.

At four, he does not understand
the subtle vocabulary of prejudice:
cycling on the adjacent street without a shirt,
black hair falling in ringlets around his face,
the voices of mothers holding summer drinks
and their children laughing inside the castle,
the sounds carry over such that, for months after,
when I hear children playing,
all the darkness in my skin carries outwards
and drowns me in its riotous, unerasable pigment.
I become the beast itself, the barbarian woman –

What is your name, savage –
from which bone and skein
do you weave yourself a new body?
how do you write your history
on this heavy continent?

If the space

between Michael and Mikhail,
Nasrani and Nazarene,
Coptic and Qibti,
Yaum-e-Ashurah and Yom Kippur,
Isaac and Ishaq,
Moses and Musa, Boabdil and Abu Abdullah,
Al-Khazar and Alcázar,
dakaait and dacoit,
looter and lotera,
shampoo and champoo –
if the space between
an English rose and an Arab rose,
a Turkish tulip and a Dutch tulip,
and the space between Burberry and Lahori lawn
is the space between qaaf and 'k'
and if I subtract 'J' from Joseph and turn it to Yusuf,
then the space between Adam and Aadam
and Daud and David decreases to almost a hair's breadth,
the space between balmy and sunny,
melancholia and depression, and the space between
holy water and ittar fits into a pendant
because the space between a necklace and a taweez
is the space between a Rumi verse and a Rumi meme,

and the space between Indian brown and Pakistani brown
would make the space between Cain and Cabeel
and Abel and Habeel grow sleeker, so the space
would not matter; the distance, a centimetre;
the sounds would collapse, the colonizer colonized,
and yet, in the space between Zul Kifl and Ezekiel
and Enoch and Idrees
and in the space between Shalom Aleichem
and Salam Alaikum, olives fell from heavy trees,
and barbed wire sunk its teeth into our spleens
so we became botched translations of ourselves,
heathens, although we were believers.
The doors of the mezquita closed
and they rewrote the Kufic epitaphs in Latin;
the doors of the Hagia Sophia closed
and they rewrote Latin epitaphs in Kufic.

In the morning

there are tulips in bloom in the north.
Sunlight pours into the crevices,
bleaches the wrinkles;
strangers soften the tissue
which appears curvaceous and round.
The nose becomes adorable, a stub,
the eyebrows shoot up in surprise,
and the smile lines return, like well-trod paths
lined with wildflowers, paths for walking
but not getting lost in.
My forehead gleams like a library stacked with books,
dusty volumes crumble onto my face,
silverfish and mothballs
the detritus of a sound education
collects on the bridge of my nose,
my glasses are rose-tinted,
a dewdrop earring catches reflections and light,
my teeth gleam and are distributed to strangers,
molars like free samples
readily entrusted into the hands
and purses of strangers,
but at night I am the southern continent,
the European unconscious,

a sea of incoherence rises to disfigure me.
In the mirror of the colonial
I am still an animal;
I am the cold of underground subways,
the slithering shadows of empty train stations.
My eyes collect darkness around the edges.
In the bus driver's rear-view mirror,
I see myself and feel afraid.

Fathers

who are dying in the motherland
aren't imaginable anymore.
Their cancer is an unrecognizable voice
on the phone that quivers and shakes –
who are you, and what have you done with him?

The plant has been growing for years now
and you have watered it and nourished it
and by God, it is enormous now.

If you hadn't left, had never got a visa,
if you had never received admission,
if you had never been away,
if he had got help a year earlier,
if the rains, if climate change,
if the air quality,
if the marriage had not soured,
if I had been there –

The plant has seized your throat.

But he wanted you to go, and he was proud.
It is so hard to make fathers proud,
let alone dying fathers in home countries
where you have left them behind.

The plant is putting sharp little feelers
into your heart. It has found large reserves
of watery, silver shame to grow into.
There is much for it to thrive in.

Why did you leave? Why do you stay?
You fly in to fly out, you left him to know him,
and you knew him so you left him
and now he speaks in a voice that's not his own
and you sit in the shade of the plant
that is a tree
that is the universe.

Bookcase

There are miles between us, though we are speaking;
behind you, a thousand friends, the gleaming bookcase.

You talk down to me and I accept this honour, for there are
seven single-author monographs in your bookcase.

You laugh at my misuse of punctuation; *Racism,
materiality and meta-reality*, says a title in the bookcase.

You say, 'Does Punjabi have this many commas?'
as if a distant language is responsible for my disasters.

You've had a new book proposal accepted: *Marginalities
within Academia*, a future entrant in the bookcase.

I dream of panel discussions I have arranged, conferences
I have left enthralled, while my eyes gaze over the bookcase.

48

'I appreciate how the chapters are coming together,' you say,
while I notice you have colour-coded your bookcase.

It's been four years and I don't have the first draft,
while you're re-arranging the books in your bookcase.

You insist on a supervisor-supervisee coffee but don't show up;
I am haunted by the empty cups of tea on your bookcase.

I refresh my browser, for the date for my thesis defense,
a dissertation proudly displayed in your bookcase.

You use my main hypothesis in your new work,
cite brown women I want to carve into the bookcase.

If I don't get a job, I will apply to clean in this department,
and every night I will dust this bookcase.

Passport Skin

I

Back when you were green and printed on cheap paper
we would speak to each other,
marvel at the signs of journeys made.
I caressed the seeping ink from a single-entry visa
to countries that would still accept you as you were.
You could never travel to Jerusalem
and this never bothered you until Abe Lincoln
spread his arms and invited you to the promised land.
Year after year, one shining sticker replaced another
and your body learnt the privilege of mobility
without fear of consequence, but your photograph
remained bare-boned, watermarked, badly lit like mine.

One day you got that entry stamp into Lahore airport
and I hoped that Capitol Hill had not made you forget
the paper of your people. But you remained
much the same, your quality undegraded.
I did not know that your visas were fiction,
like your fine Aryan nose, Queen's English
and Ivy League education: these could not overcome
the movement of data in a server

at the bottom of the ocean floor,
trickling algorithms within narrow capillaries
which could burst at any moment
because of your strange Muslim name,
neutral expression, and permitted religious headgear.
Your passport was a dangerous book of spells;
though you trapped so many fireflies in it.
You were forced to return to your parent's home,
which still smelled the same,
and you felt both forty and sixteen.

Your face would not be stamped
for many years afterwards, except with fine lines;
and in the passport, visas that had been pure magic,
providing succour to the dreams of émigrés,
slowly expired, became invalid.
Concertina wire grew around
Its beautiful golden body like a briar rose.

II

I thought I could weave myself a new skin
but my passports grate against each other;
they do not create an ombre, but a scab.
How many permits do I need, how many stamped visas
till I become another creature altogether,
translucent, twirling across security checks?

I cover my body in paper, but I moult under questioning:
What is your language? Is it Dari?
How do we get to the root of your category,
the bottom of this hybrid mess?
How do we find the bone beneath the scab –
they tear away the protective layer, the onerous cargo
that is colour, Islam, race, gender, the things
I always have to tuck into a suitcase, roll into my shoes,
so they won't break on a clean airport floor
and create a scene.

                    No matter what I do,
the Muslim woman in me appears on the scanner,
the mysterious creature covered from head to toe
in whispering scripts, swathed in sacred pashmina
and beaded black oppression.

They will find her,
however much she tries to be another thing:
contorting belly dancer, fertile, semi-literate,
belligerent, indecipherable, distant, sexual,
asexual, esoteric, devout temptress, fanatical,
men's pet, smoky-eyed, deer-pupilled,
illegal alien – her, with Arabic on her skin,
Dari on her belly.

They keep finding her.
I am tired of fighting her. I will paint myself
an empty signifier, adorn my belly with beads,
move my hips till this poem implodes
with the sound of jewellery.

Paris Proper

I went to Paris but we were in two different cities:
she in Paris Proper, and I
in the city-within-the-city,
a ruination two stops away from the Louvre.

She saw warm crepes with jam,
and cold newlyweds with beautiful shoulders,
striking brave poses against mighty gusts of wind
at the Tour De Eiffel.
I saw Pakistanis, North Africans,
in frayed jackets, dirty mufflers,
selling plastic tat, keychains,
reproductions of the tower for a euro,
hawking yesterday's *Le Monde,*
their bodies dancing a different tango
from the dancers by the Seine.

At Musée d'Orsay, she was surrounded by
Monet's water lilies, Degas's ballerinas,
and Renoir's little blonde girls –
but I couldn't get the bust of a Sudanese man
with a turban, by Charles Cordier,
out of my mind.

It saturated the air:
a nameless knock-off,
his body an ethno-object,
a curiosity in the gallery,

Louis-Bouchard's Egyptians
traipsed over the marble floor,
The representation that we crave?
My foremothers dancing,
long-sleeved, cotton-skirted,
gyrating, belly-dancing,
in front of a rabid, lazy, hook-nosed king.
Under it, my body,
not knowing what to do with itself.

As objects, what did they feel?
As subjects, in a Frenchman's wet dream?

Broken Up

Travellers in Albaicín gather in the afterglow.
The tourists are taking their buses home
and the locals breathe the night air in peace.
The city sheds its pretense, the skyline cleared of bodies,
the Alhambra golden in the distance, appearing as the sun
pours its wine down the sunburnt hills.
Soon the building and the minaret begin to radiate
as though their insides might boil over with light.
Boabdil's loss seems palpable suddenly,
the gulp in his throat, the Moor's last sigh,
the final drawing of blood, the last look over the Beloved,
this home which still dazzles many hundreds of years later.
I feel his nerves rattle as night falls.

I first travelled to Granada with an old friend.
We had an ugly falling out some years ago
and now her memory is an irritant: taking pictures with her,
sharing the skyline, fumbling in our bags for snacks,
not wanting to move, feeling this evening in our bones.
I try to wrench her presence from this landscape,
make the recollection purer, but her ghost keeps walking in,
asking for a better angle in the photograph.

I plead with her to bury our inconsequential histories
in another city, an unimportant one,
perhaps that sleepy town we passed along the way.
Not here. But she plants herself into the city wall,
her arm pressing down on my shoulder until it hurts,
making sure I see her head of straightened hair
against the inky blue horizon.

Third–World Teeth

In the last weeks of pregnancy, she sees clouds the shape of embryos
and dreams repeatedly of losing all her teeth.

No matter how much she polishes her accent, how much education she amasses,
the proof is in the pudding, and the story is her teeth:

each one mishapen, potholes in the road, broken molars,
fillings of old metal, never regularly cleaned, the alignment all wrong.

'Have you considered getting braces?' the dentist asks Shireen, aged thirty,
the wrong decade to be fixing a row of protruding teeth.

'And when was the last time you had them cleaned? A year ago? Two?'
She did not know that there were things to be done about teeth.

She had her first cavity at twelve; the dentist poked at it but never filled it.
'Here's some chewing gum,' she said, 'for the soreness of teeth.'

Named after the beloved, for her Farhad, sliced open a mountain and made a river of milk.
Queen of nowhere, now the only crown she has is placed on her teeth.

'Inside the immigrant's mouth,' says the dentist, 'is the European dream.
Here in the decaying molars, a generation of infected gums, aching teeth.

These non-pearly whites will outlive us, flesh and sinew turning to dust,
but – left undisturbed – these storied teeth, smaller than beetles, stay sharp.'

Let me close my mouth, conclude this poem first, dentist.
And in the meantime, forget everything and bleach my teeth.

Dear Susanne

I thought I'd write you this letter,
to say the things I didn't get a chance to say on the bus.
We were in a hurry, there was a deep sadness in your eyes
that threw me, and honestly I was more fixated
on which bus stop was next, for I am afraid, terrified
of getting lost in this city, but I digress.
What I wanted to say was this:
I will come to your Christmas dinner
and sit across from you at the table.
It is most unfair to go through life
when your friends have died,
to have one less at the table each year, one less toast,
one less present to buy till there is no one left
except a stranger on a bus, who seems more interested in
playing with the buttons on her coat.
I will be pleased to share a meal with you
and hear your stories. You're right –
the rain does add to the loneliness. I agree with you.
I am keeping an eye out for you while I wait
at Aegidmarkt for Bus 605. I am saving you a spot
on the bench and one on the bus.
Till later, friend.
Yours, Rakhshan.

Something New

A shadowy door.
In the distance, the body anointed with divine perfume,
arabesques dancing on the walls.

A man in a lab coat, his hands cold.
He says something, but his voice is a distant song,
the chill of his hands on my body.

I push him away, so they hold me down.
He doesn't like me, I know, the animal in me is telling me.
I tell my husband, who looks at a spot on the wall.

Iqra! Read, O Prophet, in the Name of your Lord
Who created – created humans from a clinging clot.
He takes a step back, the small man.

There is a vial in his hands: liquid that he is going to push
into my spine with a needle. I shake my head,
but it seems that language has left me.

'You're wearing too many clothes,' he says.
'Sorry,' he says, unhooking my bra.
My spine is as icy as everything now.

The blood cools; his features become muddled.
He is creatural, a pen pushed behind his ear,
melting into the lobe.

If I take enough notes, on how he is, how he moves
I can write a poem about this later,
how on birthing tables, we become things.

They're saving our life, you see; they don't have to be nice,
while they do it, survival is key, not dignity.
'You're moving too much,' the surgeon says.

The nurse with the ventouse pump beckons,
the baby's shape bruised, conical.
A foggy light appears in the corridor.

I step out of bed hoping to find my old body,
but instead collapse on the white tiles,
wake up at the end of a time-lapse video.

'You were so brave,' someone says. She pulls up a stool.
I sit and let warm water beat down on my back,
uneven hands making me into something new.

Caucasity

A latecomer at a postcolonial perspectives on cosmopolitanism conference,
I make myself invisible. This should be easy, since I have spent the last decade
learning the skill of artful disappearance.

The crowd is a sea of academics in black jackets. Nobody turns, because I am quiet,
and I seat myself in the last row, but a pair of blue eyes, offended by this interruption,
this melanin for his gaze, this unpleasant offering, fixates on my face.

Instead of staring back, I look away, pretend that none of this is happening,
that if I don't acknowledge the exclusion, it didn't happen.
Like I have to sign off on racism before it becomes real.

And so I tear up the contract: find a spot on the wall,
a shady corner, a leaf in the wind, a grey tile, stare at white academics
presenting papers on postcoloniality, and how it applies to their nation-states.

I do a quick scan of the room. As prey, my mind constantly navigates the thread of predators who don't kill but casually humiliate, which is much worse.

I come to the conclusion that I am one of two people of colour in the room.

The other brown woman is in the front row: a distinguished guest, an invited speaker (unlike my small, unwanted, doctoral ass), listening to all this with a dour expression, not looking to massage anyone's ego, to please or disarm anyone.

After the presentation on postcoloniality in Denmark, it is her turn to present: 'If someone had told me this was the white postcolonialism conference, I wouldn't have put in a paper.' Nobody laughs, but she does, rather loudly.

Any questions? The blue-eyed man says, 'I don't understand how coloniality is only valid for certain countries. For example, Germany was ruled by the Roman Empire. Surely colonialism and empire is part of everyone's history?'

'Does anyone here have lived experience of living under the Roman Empire?' she says.

'Does anyone here have lived experience of living under the British Empire?'

I raise a reluctant hand.

'There you go!' she says, with a soft movement of the hand
and then continues with the rest of her paper. In that moment, I am glad to exist
and to come into view briefly if only to prove her point.

Melting Pot/Salad Bowl

Sufis in the dervish lodge
spin incantations,
planets in their orbits,
Hazrat Yusuf said he saw a dream in which
the moon and the stars traced paths around him,
Abraham in Mecca
circumambulated around the Kabah,
Hajrah's postpartum wife ran
from one hill to the other,
hungry infant on her breast –
into this soup, history, the ladle,
the boundaries faded,
coins in the funnel spinning
in the centre of the yolk,
things fall apart,
in the centripetal fold
this tortuous commotion,
the west's gravitational pull
is strong, pulling our bodies from our homes,
and our beds, separating us from our lovers,
unlocking our lips from a mediocre kiss,
pied piper of social mobility,
beguiling us into the melting pot

or was it the salad bowl,
a type of delectable meal anyway,
we fall headlong, all of us,
ancestors and predecessors,
generations, ovum, geriatric eggs,
we rub our melanin on other skins
and they on ours,
the attraction is strong and the floor collapses,
into the core dropping further still,
there are those for whom this is a colossal mess
of epic proportions
and they will put their hands
into this abominable salad
and separate the lettuce from the tomatoes,
wanting to share the dressing with
only certain turgid, organic ones,
not wanting a piece of that exotic okra,
or the odd-looking beet, the odiferous ginger
and the introverted garlic,
nor the onion, the hypocrite,
paneer even though he is white-passing,
cilantro, the deceptive foreign cousin of parsley,
mint, the alpha, green chilli,
the sly aubergine, the insecure phallus.

Seville

The whole city can be eaten:
there are ten frozen yoghurt places dotting the street,
and the Alcazar is basically a layer cake,
history one layer of cream cheese frosting
between two layers of sponge.

On one floor: open archways and calligraphy,
the Mudejar motto inscribed on the walls in royal blue,
the fountain playing outside, the water emerald green,
a calm shrubbery adjacent to the water,
strutting peacocks and cool silences, muqarnas,
honeycomb roof rendered in gold and bronze,
the shadow of palm trees falling on the sand-
   coloured corridors.

On the second floor, the designs are austere,
the opulence replaced with scarcity:
gothic ceilings and oil paintings of Peter of Castile,
and a stern-looking monk hung from the walls,
nativity scenes, an opulent fresco,
and chandeliers shining on a chessboard floor.

Both layers rest against each other,
angry lovers who do not kiss

but must cohabit still.
The separation of history into distinct floors,
as if this were possible to do with ourselves:
separate the Indian Lucknow from the Punjabi Lahore
and the Germanic European –
let them each rest a safe distance from each other.
In this quaint house, go up the steps
to feel more European,
come down the stairs
to feel more Arab,
and linger in between
to feel a bit of each.

ABOUT THE POET

Rakhshan Rizwan works as an Acquisitions Editor. She has a PhD in Comparative Literature from Utrecht University.

Her poetry pamphlet, *Paisley* (The Emma Press, 2017) was shortlisted for the Saboteur Award and the Michael Marks Poetry Prize.

Her collection of children's poetry, *My Sneezes are Perfect* (The Emma Press, 2021) documents the difficulties of moving countries, and living through a pandemic from the perspective of a young child.

Her book *Kashmiri Life Narratives: Human Rights, Pleasure, and the Local Cosmopolitan* (Routledge, 2020) looks at how Kashmiri authors use innovative languages of happiness to do human rights advocacy.

Her writing has appeared in *Aaduna, Nimrod, Postcolonial Text* and *Blue Lyra Review*, among others. She is on the editorial team of the children's poetry journal *Tyger Tyger Magazine*.

She is from Lahore, Pakistan, has lived in Germany and the Netherlands, and currently lives in the Bay Area of North California, US.

ABOUT THE ILLUSTRATOR

Reena Makwana is a London-based illustrator who creates illustrations using drawings, embroidery and print. Her work is influenced by the city, characters, creatures, social past and present. She has produced work for clients including *Vittles, Pit Magazine, Endeavour Agency, Lecker, Big Family Press, OOMK* and *At The Table.*

Paisley

Poems by Rakhshan Rizwan,
with an introduction by Leila Aboulela

Rakhshan Rizwan's debut pamphlet simmers with a poised, driving anger. Drawing on the rich visual and material culture of her home region, Rizwan unpacks and offers critical comment on the vexed issues of class, linguistic and cultural identity – particularly for women – in the context of Pakistan and South Asia.

*Shortlisted for Best Poetry Pamphlet in
the 2018 Michael Marks Awards.*

'Rakhshan Rizwan impresses with an alert and peripatetic poetic consciousness.' - Sabotage Reviews

'There is fierce energy here, and uncompromising intensity.' - Sphinx

Print ISBN 978-1-910139-78-3

My Sneezes Are Perfect

POEMS BY RAKHSHAN RIZWAN, WITH YUSUF SAMEE
ILLUSTRATED BY BENJAMIN PHILLIPS

What's your favourite food? Who's your best friend?
Have you tried to grow a rock? Aren't beards weird?
Did you ever move house and miss your old home?
Didn't a lot change when the pandemic started?

My Sneezes Are Perfect is a collection of poems in the
voice of a small boy who wants to tell you about all the
things he's learning, all the time. During the book, he
moves from the Netherlands to America and has to
adjust to his new life there. Then Covid-19 hits and his
world changes all over again...

Print ISBN 978-1-912915-68-2
Poems aimed at children aged 8+

ABOUT THE EMMA PRESS

The Emma Press is an independent publishing house based in the Jewellery Quarter, Birmingham, UK. It was founded in 2012 by Emma Dai'an Wright, and specialises in poetry, short fiction and children's books.

The Emma Press has been shortlisted for the Michael Marks Award for Poetry Pamphlet Publishers in 2014, 2015, 2016, 2018, and 2020, winning in 2016.

In 2020 The Emma Press received funding from Arts Council England's Elevate programme, developed to enhance the diversity of the arts and cultural sector by strengthening the resilience of diverse-led organisations.

Website: theemmapress.com
Facebook, Twitter and Instagram:
@TheEmmaPress